Some Woman
Had to Fight

The Radical Life of Sue Shelton White

Gay Majure Wilson

Illustrations by Will Wilson

For my mother, born just 10 years after women won their equal right to vote, for showing her daughter the strength and fortitude of an independent woman.

If you stand in your accepted place today, some woman had to fight yesterday, and we should be a bit ashamed to stand on ground won by women in the past without making some effort to honor them by winning a higher and wider field for the future.

Sue Shelton White

Contents

CHAPTER 1

Rowdyism About to Break Loose

In 1915 the world heaved under the strain of war and tragedy. World War I raged in Europe. The British ocean liner Lusitania was attacked and sunk by a German U-boat's torpedo. A deadly hurricane struck Galveston for the second time in the new century, taking hundreds of lives and devastating the Texas coastline, while the menace of Typhoid Mary struck in New York.

There were moments of distraction and optimism. Babe Ruth hit his first home run. Americans witnessed the first coast-to-coast phone call, between Alexander Graham Bell in New York and his assistant Thomas Watson in San Francisco.

The year also brought suffrage gains for women in Denmark and Iceland.[1,2] But women in the United States of America still were fighting for recognition of their right to vote.

In October 1915 the Tennessee Equal Suffrage Association held its state convention in Jackson, Tennessee, where 28-year-old Sue Shelton White worked as a stenographer, a job she had inherited from her older sister Lucy. Lucy had left behind small-town life for the glamor of being a newspaper reporter in San Francisco.

White was born 20 miles away in Henderson, Tennessee on May 25, 1887. Her father was a lawyer and preacher. Her mother taught music lessons to local children. Both died when White was young, thrusting the burdens of self-sufficiency upon young Sue and her siblings at an early age.[3]

White was named recording secretary of the Tennessee suffrage association at the 1915 convention. The local suffragists urged Tennessee state legislators to vote for equal suffrage, but also expressed appreciation to President Woodrow Wilson for endorsing voting rights for women.[4] How things would change just two years later.

In November 1917 nationally known and often reviled suffragists Maud Younger and Mrs. Howard Gould drove across the American South on a lecture tour. Calling it the *Dixie Tour*, Younger and Gould lectured in the Southern states to promote the causes of the National Woman's Party (NWP). As they traveled, they were caught in the political crossfire over the NWP's public protests in Washington, D.C. The Dixie Tour sought to defend the defiant protests, which were under attack as being unpatriotic during the crisis and horror of World War I.[5]

Younger was from California. Gould was from New York. Upon arriving in the South, they were strangers in a strange land. After stops in Alabama and Georgia, Younger and Gould headed to Tennessee.

Becky Hourwich Reyher was a young college student from New York who had married earlier that year. As an organizer for the NWP, she was one of several women sent ahead of Younger and Gould to the Southern states. This was Reyher's first long trip away from home. Anger toward the NWP's militant suffragists was mounting as she traveled through each state. "And now it was getting hot and sharp in Tennessee," she reported.

Reyher arrived in Jackson, Tennessee to meet officials and arrange permission for the lecture stop in this small city in West Tennessee surrounded by cotton fields. "We had no Committee women in Jackson. . .I was entirely alone."

Reyher had an appointment to meet the Jackson mayor. She stopped on a downtown street and asked "a nice, sweet looking woman" for directions. The local newspaper had carried Reyher's photo and a story of her arrival. The woman recognized her: "You are one of the suffragists, aren't you?" Reyher confirmed yes. The woman replied, "Good luck to you."

Reyher later needed to dictate a report of her work and send it to renowned NWP leader Alice Paul. She went to the office of a public stenographer who the hotel staff had recommended: "Miss Sue, the best one in town."

When Reyher arrived at the stenographer's office, she was surprised to find that it was the same sweet, helpful woman she had spoken with earlier on the street — Sue Shelton White.

Reyher confided to White that the mayor was having doubts about allowing the lecture. Rumors were swirling that local residents were threatening trouble, with some demanding that the suffragists be run out of town. "Sue listened, her eyes flashing."

White called the mayor and police chief. She demanded that the suffragist leaders be allowed to speak and that city officials protect them from harm. White assured the mayor that she could vouch for the suffragists and their message. She argued that these women simply were asking for the vote, and nothing about that could be called unpatriotic.

City officials relented and gave their permission.

Younger and Gould arrived in Jackson on November 22, 1917. Younger sported a flowing chiffon dress and decorative, wide-brimmed hat. Reyher later recalled, "The whole town was agog."

That evening White spoke first to the audience of 250. Reyher recalled, "I was surprised to hear the deep rumble that came from that slender frame, or the passion and oratory with which her words rolled out." White reminded the audience to show their Southern hospitality to the visitors. Two burly men walked the aisle ready to arrest troublemakers, with "the atmosphere of rowdyism about to break loose."[6]

Younger spoke passionately about the federal suffrage amendment and defended the NWP's tactic of picketing the White House.

After Younger's lecture, the Jackson audience passed a resolution asking the mayor of Nashville, Tennessee to grant Younger permission to speak in his city. The resolution vouched that Younger had said nothing unpatriotic or disloyal about the United States or the President. It was signed by five leading citizens of Jackson: a banker, a newspaper owner and secretary of the Jackson Association of Commerce, an attorney, the chief of police, and meeting chairman Sue Shelton White.[7]

White is credited by Reyher with transforming the atmosphere of that controversial meeting. "She spellbound that hostile audience. The rumblings stopped, the atmosphere became friendly. . .We hated to leave Jackson."

After the meeting, White told the suffragists she would

accompany them and smooth the way on their tour through Tennessee. "And everywhere, thanks to her, the hostility vanished."[8]

White relied on her work as a stenographer to make her living as a single woman in the early 20th century. By closing her office to join the suffragist tour, she knew that she was sacrificing the financial stability her job brought. It was the first of many risky career moves, of which White would say, "I am not afraid of starving."[9]

When Reyher returned to Washington, she and Younger both told Alice Paul about White. "It was then Miss Paul began badgering Sue to come to Washington, and you know the rest," Reyher wrote years later.[10]

That tense, unpredictable evening in her hometown marked White's debut on the national suffragist stage.

CHAPTER 2

Every Mother's Daughter

In 1917, during World War I, the National Woman's Party was reviled by many for daring to stage militant protests in Washington, D.C. in a time of war.

Writing to a Tennessee newspaper in November 1917, White defended the White House pickets by the NWP, arguing that women of gentle breeding and high ideals were picketing on behalf of "their leader, Alice Paul, who is dying in the Occoquan Workhouse,"[1] an odious place known for its brutal treatment and forced feedings of suffragist prisoners.

The newspaper editor replied, insisting that the NWP's militant methods were costing the suffrage movement the empathy of the nation, at a time when the country faced its greatest crisis. The editor pointed to the ability of the other, quieter faction of the suffragists — the National Woman's Suffrage Association — to "present their cause without ill feeling."[2]

Less than two years later, on February 9, 1919, White was center stage in the protests. She was among almost 100 women who marched to the White House and gathered shoulder to shoulder around an urn. A curious crowd of several thousand people had gathered, standing for two hours, listening and watching the spectacle in anxious anticipation of what may come next.

A fire was lit. Flames leapt skyward. White held high the words of an unfulfilled pledge by President Wilson to extend democracy to women — then dropped the pledge in the fire — her anger burning at his empty promises. A cartoon three-foot paper effigy of Wilson also went up in flames.[3]

White and 64 other women were arrested by civil and military police. After the principal speaker Mrs. Henry O. Havemeyer was arrested, more women dashed to the podium to speak in her place. Each was grabbed and arrested as she made her desperate attempt. The women kept up their protests and shouted at spectators as they were shoved into patrol wagons.[4]

At the police station, the women refused to post bond and were jailed. White served five days in the filthy, harsh conditions of the Lorton Women's Workhouse in Virginia.

The arrests of the suffragists brought mixed reactions in White's hometown. The editor of a neighboring small-town newspaper complained:

The female nuisances who made themselves conspicuous and offensive by picketing the White House for the purpose of annoying the President and members of his cabinet are just where they ought to be—in jail—and should be allowed to remain there until they promise, and make bond if necessary, to go to their homes, where they are doubtless of minimum use —and God pity the men they go back to.[5]

The Tennessee Suffrage Association — the moderate faction of the suffragists — opposed the White House pickets, claiming they were unpatriotic.[6]

After her release, White joined other former prisoners aboard the *Prison Special* train tour in February and March 1919. It was a cross-country speaking tour by 26 former suffragist prisoners to publicize their brutal, unjust experience and recruit supporters for the NWP.[7]

As she traveled, White proudly wore the silver pin of a jail door awarded by the NWP to her and the other women for their suffering and sacrifice.

A Nashville newspaper announced:

Prison Special on Way—Our Sue Aboard. The "prison special" is off—Sue White is on, and O boy, they are Nashville bound! No member of the party of the special has anything about her resembling green. They are hard-boiled—tough—stickers, and every mother's daughter of the whole bunch has been on the inside looking out. They are coming! Legislators, look out![8]

A month later, in April 1919, the Tennessee legislature was locked in a contentious three-hour debate over a statewide suffrage bill that would allow Tennessee women to vote in elections for President and Vice President of the United States and for local municipal offices.

The emotional words of Sen. Lonsdale P. McFarland brought some suffragists to tears during the long, heated debate. He argued that if a man would trust a woman with his name, his honor and the rearing of his children, there was no reason why he should not trust her with the ballot. He insisted that woman was the equal of man in peace and in war.

Sen. J. Parks Worley led the opposition to the bill, claiming that he was speaking for the women who were not present, but who were at home attending to their duties there. He claimed that 90 percent of the women in Tennessee were opposed to equal suffrage and that the other 10 percent were deluded. Sen. Worley compared the suffragists to "cruel rulers" like Catherine the Great of Russia and Elizabeth I of England.

Sen. Ernest N. Haston previously had opposed the suffragist bill, but changed his mind and planned to vote in favor of its passage. Sen. Worley mockingly asked Sen. Haston if the light that he had seen to change his mind was like that seen by St. Paul on the road to Damascus — or rather the light of the fire used by Sue White to burn President Wilson's words.

His caustic remarks were met with a chorus of hisses and boos from the suffragists in the chamber's gallery. They were reprimanded and threatened to be evicted. Sen. Worley tried to twist their meaning, saying that he did not blame the women for hissing at the name of White.

Sen. E.E. Patton declared that Sue White was not a true representative of the suffragists and that President Wilson was in favor of suffrage, "even if he had been abused by Miss White and her kind."

After the debate, the Senate chamber fell silent for the roll call. Anticipation and anxiety hung in the air. Sixteen senators voted aye in favor of passage. Only three senators remained — two of them known opponents of the suffrage bill. All eyes and ears were on the third and final vote — Sen. Wikle — as he finally spoke, with trepidation in his voice: "Mr. Speaker, the vote I am about to cast today may be cause for regret someday, but I am going to vote aye."

The Senate chamber erupted in cheers. The suffragists surrounded Sen. Wikle with adulation for his deciding vote. The suffrage bill had passed by a slim majority of 17 to 14.[9] Tennessee women now could vote in limited elections. They still could not hold public office.

A year later White was 32 years old and living at the NWP headquarters in Washington, D.C., sharing the residence with 11 other suffragists. The 1920 census listed her home as "Women Suffragist Club" and her occupation as "Organizer."[10]

In September 1920 Alice Paul sent White back to her home state to open the NWP's Nashville headquarters. White's job was to direct the fight in Tennessee for ratification of the Nineteenth Amendment:

The right of citizens of the United States to vote shall not be denied or abridged by the United States or by any State on account of sex.

The Tennessee vote was crucial. It was the only way that the amendment would be ratified in time for women to vote in the November presidential election. White would have home turf advantage, and Paul knew it. While in Tennessee, White stayed in constant touch with Paul in Washington to devise a winning

19

strategy.

"She worked at white heat, directing the lobbyists, day by day, and hour by hour, so that at every moment they knew where the Amendment stood in the Legislature,"[11] recalled Florence Armstrong, a government economist who first met White through their jobs and became her loyal partner during the last decade of White's life.

The persistent, tireless lobbying brought victory for the suffragists and all women. On August 18, 1920, Tennessee became the 36th state to ratify the Nineteenth Amendment. Women across the country soon would be voting for the 29th President of the United States.

More than 20 years later, *The New York Times* credited White for the crucial victory in Tennessee:

In 1920 Miss White led a successful battle to persuade the Tennessee Legislature to adopt the constitutional amendment giving women the right of suffrage. Tennessee was one of the last states to vote upon the question, its approval permitting women all over the United States to vote in the Presidential election that year.[12]

With the amendment ratified, White returned to her adopted home of Washington, D.C.

Five years later she was sent to Tennessee again. In July 1925 White left Washington and returned to Jackson at the direction of Alice Paul to investigate a run for the U.S. Congress. Paul saw that the Democratic Party had nominated only two women for the U.S. Congress and the Republicans had nominated none. She was determined to change that.

Rumors spread in Tennessee that White planned to mount a run against U.S. Representative Gordon Browning of the 8th District — her home district — if she found the political environment favorable for her candidacy.[13] Ultimately, White did not run, and Browning represented the 8th District for 10 years.

In 1929 the bright lights and boisterous revelry of the Roaring Twenties abruptly ended. The stock market crashed, and the Jazz Age gave way to the Great Depression. It was a time of dramatic change for the country and for White. She said her farewells and ended her 12-year relationship with the National Woman's Party.

CHAPTER 3

Some Woman Had to Fight

"The best way to find yourself is to lose yourself in the service of others." — Mahatma Gandhi

White's life was a testament to her devotion to the service of others. She fought for the causes and people she championed, especially those who were overlooked or mistreated.

She was proud of her appointment as executive secretary to the Tennessee Commission for the Blind. Her job was to educate Tennesseans on how to help the blind become independent and self-sufficient.[1] White appreciated the growing importance of this mission as the lasting tragedies of World War I permeated the nation. Soldiers were returning home sightless from their battle injuries. They were suffering the effects of post-traumatic stress disorder in a time before it was fully understood and diagnosed. Physicians and the public labeled them *shell shocked*. These war veterans needed new skills and purpose.

In December 1917 Tennessee established an industrial school for the blind. White sent letters in November 1918 encouraging people to purchase the brooms the students were making, urging Tennesseans to "help the blind help themselves" and guaranteeing a good-quality broom in return.[2]

White also battled for the rights of consumers. "A slow and steady fight is meat and drink to Miss Sue White" proclaimed the headline as White began organizing consumer councils for President Franklin D. Roosevelt's New Deal.[3] "Word got around that nobody cares about the consumer, and Sue White was right at the side of Mrs. Mary Rumsey heading the consumers' cause."[4]

An experimental program, these volunteer consumers' councils were formed in 200 counties across the country to watch for price fixing and gouging. The councils were short-lived, and White grew frustrated with cuts to the program's funding and dwindling influence within Roosevelt's administration. She ultimately resigned.[5]

White argued for the rights of women in the federal work force. She won the right for women in the Federal Civil Service to continue to use their own name on the payroll after they married.[6]

White fought for the rights of early 20th century

businesswomen. In 1929 she was elected president of the Jackson Business and Professional Women's Club. In her first speech, she declared:

If you stand in your accepted place today, some woman had to fight yesterday, and we should be a bit ashamed to stand on ground won by women in the past without making some effort to honor them by winning a higher and wider field for the future. It is our business. It is a debt we owe. . .No matter what may be the place you hold, it is not secure to you except by the concerted effort of women. . .We must remember the past, hold fast to the present and build for the future. [7]

Late in her career, as a federal attorney, White lost an opportunity to fight for the rights of children. She was in line for appointment to the bench of the District of Columbia Juvenile Court, succeeding Judge Kathryn Sellers. The society editor of a Tennessee newspaper endorsed White for the judicial appointment, declaring she would "bring to this important office a well-balanced mind and charming personality."[8]

Judge Sellers was the first federally appointed female judge in the United States, having been nominated by President Wilson in 1918. Sellers retired in 1934 following a broken hip. Like White, Sellers had obtained her law degree from the Washington College of Law and was active in the suffrage movement.[9,10]

White's proposed judicial appointment was opposed by the Women's Trade Union League. White's partner Armstrong later said this opposition was due to a misunderstanding of White's attitude toward labor and called it a great loss to the court:

Her logical mind, her knowledge of law enforcement, her compassion, her practical sense, her magnetic personality, her balancing sense of humor, and the ability to lift and inspire others…might have made her a great judge in the handling of the problems of offending children.[11]

CHAPTER 4

Not Such a White Elephant

By December 1920, White had joined the office of U.S. Senator Kenneth McKellar as assistant secretary.[1] She effectively was the Tennessee senator's chief of staff — managing his mail, taking phone calls and meeting with visitors.

While working full-time for McKellar by day, White studied law by night at the Washington College of Law, the first law school founded by women.

By June 1925, White was a law school graduate, but still working for McKellar.[2] At the same time, Matthew Hale was restarting his law practice in Washington, D.C. and New York.

A graduate of Harvard Law School, Hale had practiced interstate commerce law and was a Boston alderman prior to World War I. After the war, he worked in shipping as vice president of Liberty Shipbuilding Company and president of the

South Atlantic Maritime Corp.[3] But his shipping business floundered, and he decided to return to his first calling.

In 1925 Hale approached White to join his fledgling law practice. White wrote to Sen. McKellar about the job offer: "As you know, the shipping business has sent many people on the rocks, and Mr. Hale has gone with the rest."

She noted that Hale had no capital to restart his practice, but he was looking for a partner he could trust. White acknowledged the risk of this venture, but also the potential reward if the practice was successful. "The difficulty with women trying to practice law is to make a good connection above that of a clerk, and this is what I have wanted to avoid, because I am too old to get much beyond the law-clerk stage if I start there."

She sought McKellar's advice as her mentor and her employer. "I may want to ask you not to consider me severed from your force permanently, until I see how things work out — or perhaps I should simply leave that with you, and take the risk. I am not afraid of starving."

She said of Hale, "I had been afraid he might decide against me altogether, but maybe he thinks that in this day and time, a woman may not be such a white elephant, after all, in a law organization."[4]

McKellar advised her that it was a good opportunity. He said he would regret losing her, but if she is to practice law, this may be her best chance to start.[5]

White's law partnership with Matthew Hale never materialized. Hale died weeks later — on August 29, 1925 — at 43 years old. White stayed on running Sen. McKellar's Washington office, but rough seas were on the horizon.

White was close to fellow suffragist and New York photographer Anita Pollitzer. Pollitzer was best known for her friendship with artist Georgia O'Keeffe.[6]

In December 1925 Pollitzer sent urgent telegrams to well-connected women in Nashville, asking them to wire Sen. McKellar at once to demand that he appoint White as the permanent secretary of his office. Pollitzer argued that White had been acting in the role since March and had been working diligently in McKellar's office for five years.

In her telegrams, Pollitzer wrote passionately, urging White's friends to act quickly to convince McKellar:

Ask him to consider the fact that when a woman merits promotion it is the fair thing to grant it and that Sue's friends have assumed that he would do the fair thing, knowing the high standard of her work. Say anything else you please and do so at once.[7]

She has worked hard here for five years and the promotion is due her. She naturally will not let possible discrimination because she is a woman go unchallenged. She has stood for women and women will stand for her.[8]

But White was up against a powerful force — nepotism. In a letter to White on July 6, 1926, McKellar told her:

I regret more than I can say that I am compelled to make a change in my office force. I am going to appoint, effective the 10th, my brother, Don, as my Secretary. . .Your work has been entirely satisfactory, as you know, and it is a great trial to me to have to rearrange. By December, I am sure we can work it out some way.[9]

White fired back a reply:

I was, you might say, thunderstruck to receive your letter today, and yet, all things considered, I need not have been surprised, I suppose. . .I do not know what I shall do, but will begin to look around for something. I only wish I had anticipated the situation as much as a week ago.[10]

She treaded gingerly, careful not to burn her bridges, saying that their friendship would go on regardless of their professional relationship.

A few days later, on July 14, McKellar sent an urgent telegram to White: "DON'T DO ANYTHING HASTY WE WILL WORK SITUATION OUT YET."

But the telegram was put under the wrong door at her apartment building in Washington, D.C. It was not given to her until two months later.

However, McKellar also mailed her a letter the same day he sent the wayward telegram:

I want to tell you that I regret more than I can say that you can't remain in my office. I hope we may yet work out a plan by which you may. During the seven years that you have been with me, both as clerk and Secretary, your work has been all that I could desire. You have been efficient, faithful, intelligent, energetic, and ever mindful of my best interests. No one could have done the work better. I have relied on you and never been disappointed. I have never had a more efficient employee about me, and I sincerely hope you can yet arrange some way to stay [11]

McKellar's brother Don was coming to take over the office later that fall, and McKellar was desperate for White to continue managing the office until then. White stifled her ire and remained cordial, telling McKellar she appreciated the opportunity to stay on the payroll until December.

The negotiation by mail continued. On July 19, McKellar wrote her again:

I have fully determined to bring Don to Washington just as I wrote you, and he may not understand it, but that is what will be done. That was my only reason for making any change.

I have no desire whatsoever to get rid of you, but, quite the contrary, I regret more than I can say that you will not stay with me. As I told you, I never had a better employee or one that suited me better. At present, all I can offer is what I have already offered, and I sincerely hope that you can accept it.[12]

McKellar asked her to take another position in the office and said that he would pay the difference from his own pocket to maintain her current salary.

The negotiation failed. White would not settle for less than the job she deserved — the job she already was doing — managing Sen. McKellar's Washington office as de facto chief of staff.

In November 1926 she announced she was leaving McKellar and returned to Tennessee.[13]

CHAPTER 5

A Full Partnership without Embarrassment

After working full-time managing a busy U.S. senator's office while studying nights and weekends for her law degree, White graduated in 1923 and was admitted to the bar to practice law in Tennessee.[1]

 Her 10 years in Tennessee as a stenographer and court reporter, from 1907 to 1917, were valuable training for her law studies and legal career. She had learned the complexities of the legal system and the courts. Her partner Florence Armstrong wrote years later that White's vantage point in the courtroom exposed her to the legal problems that everyday people faced. Those daily courtroom dramas reinforced her empathy and determination to fight for the underdog.[2]

Friend, colleague and former Wyoming governor Nellie Tayloe Ross later said of White, "She had the mentality and the training as a lawyer to penetrate to the heart of a difficult matter."[3]

Three years after being admitted to the bar, White lost her Washington job to Sen. McKellar's brother. But White already had begun planning for her legal career. She was 39 years old, had some cash, and was determined not to start at the bottom. In July 1926, on U.S. Senate letterhead, she wrote to highly regarded Jackson attorney Hu C. Anderson:[4]

My dear Hu –

I want you to consider this letter carefully and treat it absolutely confidential. I am on the verge of an absolute break with McKellar. It may be patched up—but I am just now considering how long before it shall come and in what way. A situation has been projected upon him which demands my sympathy but not my whole-hearted approval of the way in which it has been handled.

How is the law with you? Are you in position to take me into full partnership with you without embarrassment and on the same basis you would take on any other new person—i.e., let me put some money into the pot now. You see, I think I can raise some cash and it would probably come in handy with you. I wouldn't think of imposing myself upon you except on a business basis.

What would a fourth, say, interest in your business be, for the present, with all the energy I offer, cash down (and my moral support free of charge). I can help you now with cash, I think, and you can help me get established so I'll be independent of the whims of temperamental individuals. I would want a partnership arrangement to hold out to the public, but I am all for you and your family of course, if there's enough of your practice to keep us all.

Do some figuring and write me frankly what you think of the scheme. My salary with McKellar since Dec. has been $275.00 per month — more than the average man thinks any woman should have, I guess. I am not saying what it is now — that's one point of difference not yet settled and pending settlement it is zero.

Keep this to yourself, but write me as soon as you can.

Love, Sue

It was a brash proposal from a woman in 1926, especially in the male-dominated legal profession. She wanted a financial stake in the law firm and an equal partnership in the eyes of the public. Anderson accepted her offer, and the law firm of Anderson and White was born. White was now the first female lawyer in Jackson, Tennessee.

White's clients were often the people living in the shadows of the more rich and powerful — women or the lone figure up against a government or corporation. In divorce cases, Anderson and White mostly represented the wife, and frequently won, garnering harsh judgments against the husband:

The defendant has, in Madison County, Tennessee, been guilty of such cruel and inhuman treatment and conduct toward complainant as renders it unsafe and improper for her to cohabit with him and be under his dominion and control; that he has offered such indignities to her person as to render her condition intolerable and thereby forced her to withdraw; and that he has abandoned her and turned her out of doors and refused and neglected to provide for her and their infant child, and it further appearing that the complainant gave the defendant no cause or just excuse for his said misconduct and has not condoned the same.[5]

In this case, White's client was granted exclusive custody of her child. The husband was granted permission to visit and ordered to pay all court costs.

Some Anderson and White cases related to property rights. A local man accused a neighbor of tearing down the fence between their properties and rebuilding the fence within the border of the man's property, effectively stealing a portion of his land.[6] Anderson and White introduced the location of a cedar tree as evidence in the case and won.

They were not always the winning side. In a dispute over back taxes, Anderson and White represented 30 local residents, who were being sued by county drainage district officials. The drainage district claimed the residents owed $1,050 in delinquent taxes, interest and penalties for 1919 to 1928. Anderson and White lost the case, and the county auctioned off land owned by the defendants. The judge ordered a 77-acre tract be sold by the county clerk to the highest cash bidder on the steps of the courthouse.[7]

White was not afraid to represent small clients against big odds. She argued the case of a 41-year-old woman suing manufacturer Delco-Light Company, insurer General Motors Acceptance Corporation, and Delco's local distributor. White herself and the woman's husband posted the bond.[8]

In 1916 the Delco-Light Electric Plant generator was introduced to bring electricity and refrigeration to rural homes and farms across the country, many of which would not have electricity from a public utility until the Rural Electrification Act of 1936. Sales of the Delco-Light electric systems were booming in the late 1920s.[9]

The specifics of White's lawsuit are unknown. Perhaps it was a dispute over a defect or a warranty. White reached a settlement with the defendants on behalf of her client, and all parties agreed to dismiss the case before going to trial.

The partnership between Anderson and White would shatter less than three years after it began. Not only were they sharing a law office, but White lived with Anderson and his wife Virginia, even owning a share of their house.

Housing options for single women in 1920s Jackson were few. Sharing a house with her law partner and his wife must have been a stifling environment for White after living at the National Woman's Party headquarters in Washington years earlier, among the exuberance and camaraderie of her fellow suffragists as they plotted and struggled together for a common cause.

The house-sharing arrangement with the Andersons erupted in 1928 when White was assailed by Anderson's wife. The cause of the rift is unclear. In a December 1928 letter to Anderson and Virginia, White wrote:

Dear Friends:

The last time I had a conversation with Virginia she lost her head and became violent and threatened my life. . .I can not afford to subject myself to an environment where I must live in a room shut off from the heat in the dead of winter. If I must keep my door shut in order to avoid violence to my person or threats upon my life, or unpleasant attempts to engage me in quarrels in which I am slow to indulge, then I may as well say to you that I am through.

White said she was willing to start over and make no reference to the incident, but she would not be subjected to this treatment again. If the Andersons preferred, White was willing to give up her legal and financial claims at the office and the house. She offered to pay off her portion of the property debt and deed the house outright to Virginia.

If she stayed, White insisted, there must be civility in the home and office. "I do not care to live and to work in an environment of bitterness. Think things over and if you wish, let's talk it over — without insults."[10]

Hu and Virginia Anderson sent a curt reply. Anderson stated he was ending his professional relationship with White, but neither he nor Virginia were conceding guilt to the "very grave charges." He accepted White's offer to transfer the house title to Virginia in return for Anderson incurring the remaining debt.[11]

White moved out and offered to let the Andersons keep and use what furniture of hers they needed. She had no place to store it, and the furniture was not her priority. She asked for her books,

violin, embroidered linen
napkins, wooden candlesticks,
volumes of *Wells' Outline of
History*, and framed pictures of
the Greek temple at the San
Francisco Exposition. "While this
is all small stuff. . .some of it came to me as gifts from friends
whom I like to remember," White explained.[12]

Virginia refused to keep any of the furniture: "Dear Sue, it is
best that you remove all your things at once."[13]

White ultimately transferred her house title to Virginia, and Hu
Anderson took over White's payments on the property. The
groundbreaking law partnership of Anderson and White ended in
January 1929.

Despite the bitter ending of their personal and professional
relationship in Jackson, just two years later Anderson sought
White's help in a sensitive family matter. By that time, she had
moved back to Washington, D.C. and was working for the
Democratic National Committee.

White agreed. She did not hesitate to help her former law
partner.

Hu Anderson's stepsister Annette had been committed to St.

Elizabeth's Hospital in Washington, D.C., the first federal psychiatric hospital in the United States. Annette was working as a clerk in the office of U.S. Senator Cordell Hull from Tennessee at the time she was institutionalized.[14]

Anderson received a letter about his stepsister in December 1931 from the St. Elizabeth's superintendent:

Miss Anderson, at the time of her admission here October 6, was practically mute and appeared deeply confused. About October 23, she made a very remarkable improvement which led us to hope that she might progress rapidly toward recovery. She has, however, continued to show peculiarities and delusions, to such a degree that, as you mentioned, you have been able to discern from her writings that she is decidedly not well. She is up and about every day, keeps herself neatly clothed, does a little sewing in our occupational therapy department, enjoys somewhat the amusements and diversions provided for patients. She does not have insight concerning her mental trouble and believes, therefore, that she is now capable of returning to work. We judge from her mental condition that she would not be able to hold a position, and indeed, that it would be unwise to permit her to leave the protective environment of an institution. It is impossible to state definitely how long it will be before she will be sufficiently improved to return home and to work. At present, I should say there is not much evidence that her recovery will occur in the near future.[15]

Annette had a 4-year-old daughter, Geraldine. Annette's former husband — Geraldine's father — was absent.

Anderson sought White's help to ensure there was money available to meet young Geraldine's needs while she stayed in Washington with family friends. He sent $300 to White, equivalent to $4,600 today, asking her to manage the money primarily for the child's expenses, as well as items that Annette may need at St. Elizabeth's.

He instructed White not to give any of the money to Annette's mother Lena Anderson (his stepmother), saying it would only be wasted, probably in getting Christian Science treatment for Annette. "Money is too damn scarce to be thrown away in any such manner," Anderson complained.

Anderson used his influence with Tennessee legislators to ensure that his stepsister could stay at St. Elizabeth's indefinitely. He wrote to White:

I received a second letter from Annette which indicated very clearly to my mind that she was laboring under persecutory delusions, and was still in a very bad state mentally. In fact it was the wildest of all the letters that I have received. She is very anxious to be transferred to

Tennessee, her idea being, I am quite sure, that it would be easier to be released here. In this she is mistaken.

It is very clear that there is small hope of Annette's permanent recovery, at least any time within the near future.

Personally, I think it preposterous under present conditions to think of taking her out of an institution where she has the best care and treatment that money can afford, and transferring her to one of the State institutions where, in the very nature of things, she cannot have the consideration and care that she is now receiving gratis.[16]

White met personally with the medical staff at St. Elizabeth's on Anderson's behalf and reported back to him in Tennessee. She told Anderson that Annette had shown improvement a few weeks earlier, but the doctors reported a relapse, saying they were hesitant to call it chronic or label it as *dementia praecox*, but they feared it was. (Dementia praecox is an out-of-use term for the condition now diagnosed as schizophrenia.)

St. Elizabeth's staff told White that she should not see Annette during the visit and that Annette was not well enough to be reunited with her daughter or mother. White ended her report to Anderson, "I have given the opinion of the doctors, and have not tried to give you my opinion. Needless to say, it is with regret that

I report as I do."[17]

Another family tragedy soon followed. In 1933 Hu Anderson's stepmother Lena Anderson was struck and killed by a car at a Washington, D.C. intersection. The car was driven by the 29-year-old sister of a Florida congressman. Lena Anderson was 78 years old.

The driver, Jeanne Elizabeth Caldwell of Fresno, California, was the sister of Congressman Millard F. Caldwell of Florida. Caldwell drove the injured Anderson to the hospital and disappeared. Later she appeared at the police station with her brother, was booked, and released on bond. Lena Anderson's body was returned to Tennessee for burial.[18]

After Lena Anderson's death, daughter Annette was still institutionalized and became Washington attorney Etta L. Taggart's ward of the court. Taggart was the first woman to be admitted to the bar association in the District of Columbia.[19]

Taggart wrote to White in May 1935, asking her for funds from the money that Hu Anderson had entrusted to White for Annette and Geraldine's needs. St. Elizabeth's Hospital had written to Taggart, saying that Annette needed dresses, slips, shoes, nightgowns, and long underwear.[20]

A year later White was still helping the Anderson family. In July 1936, after Lena Anderson's estate had been settled, White delivered a package to the Hays family in Washington, D.C. It contained gold-rimmed spectacles, beaded purses, gold and silver bracelets, a pearl necklace, a cameo brooch, an Eastern Star ring, a 1916 school ring, a DAR medal, a fraternity pin and "several small broken bits of trinkets." The package also included mining, bank and mill stock certificates purchased between 1915 and 1930, valued at $3,300 at the time of purchase, but of unknown value by 1936 following the stock market crash and Great Depression.

The package was for Annette's daughter Geraldine, who was still living with the Hays' family. It was her inheritance from her late grandmother.[21]

Hu Anderson went on to become a judge in Tennessee, serving as presiding justice of the Tennessee Court of Appeals. In 1947, following World War II, he was appointed by President Harry Truman to preside at the Nuremberg trials in Germany.

Anderson was the presiding judge at the Nazi war crimes trial of Alfried Krupp von Bohlen and Halbach and other officials of the Krupp Munitions industry. The trial lasted from November 1947 to August 1948. Anderson's wife Virginia and daughter Jane

Fenn accompanied him to Germany, with his daughter acting as his secretary.[22]

Following the strain of the Nuremberg trials, Anderson returned to Jackson, Tennessee to live a quiet life as a grandfather and judge in his hometown. But tragedy would strike again.

Judge Anderson normally was the first person to arrive at the county courthouse each morning. Because the elevator operator would arrive later, Anderson would use the elevator key to take himself to his office.

In the early morning of Tuesday, May 5, 1953, the elevator operator had arrived early and taken an attorney to the third floor. While reading his newspaper, Anderson opened the elevator door and stepped into the dark, empty shaft.

He fell 30 feet to the basement of the courthouse. Anderson was conscious and able to speak after the fall. The courthouse custodian sent for his son from school. The boy crawled into the elevator shaft and tied a rope around the judge. After 20 minutes of effort, he was rescued and taken by ambulance to the hospital.

Anderson arrived with a fractured left leg, lacerations of the scalp and chin, a fracture of the lower jaw, and a possible skull fracture, although doctors did not think the skull fracture was likely. The hospital's X-ray technicians decided not to disturb

Judge Anderson until later in the day after he was rested.[23] It was a misguided decision. Hesitation sealed his fate. He died Thursday evening of a cerebral hemorrhage.

His front-page obituary in the local newspaper included the brief but memorable partnership of Anderson and White.[24]

CHAPTER 6

Two Mules

After the volatile dissolution of her law partnership with Anderson, White joined 45-year-old Jackson lawyer John F. Hall to form the law firm Hall and White. Equal billing was now a given for White. During their two-year partnership from 1929 to 1931, Hall and White cases spanned divorces to building contracts to farm animals.

As with Anderson and White, Hall and White often represented wives in divorce cases. In a 1929 case, the judge agreed that their client had suffered cruel treatment and indignities and that the husband had "contracted the habit of drunkenness since the marriage." Their client was granted the divorce she sought and "vested with all the rights of an unmarried woman and restored to the use of her maiden name."[1]

Hall and White represented a wife suing for both a divorce and

47

the husband's property — 70 acres of land, two mules, one bay horse, one yellow Jersey cow, one brindle Jersey cow, one dark red heifer, one light red heifer, a fertilizer distributor, a corn planter, a 1925 model touring car, and the household furniture.

They negotiated a cash payment for their client in lieu of the property, but the judge did not grant her the divorce. The judge concluded that the evidence was not sufficient to make the case for divorce on the grounds charged in the petition. The judge dismissed the case and ordered their client — the wife — to pay the costs of the lawsuit.[2]

Hall and White unsuccessfully represented a local contractor suing the trustees and building committee of a Methodist church for breach of contract. One of the church trustees named as a defendant in the lawsuit was the local mayor. The case was dismissed, but the judge granted the contractor's request for an appeal.[3]

Just as White was willing to do battle with politicians in the legislative arena during the suffragist campaign, she was willing to confront wealthy landowners in the courtroom. She and Hall represented local citizens suing landowners who were blocking public access to a connecting road between the landowners' properties. The outcome of the case is not known, but the townspeople had a fighter on their side with White.[4]

In another case involving farm animals, Hall and White successfully represented defendants who were being sued over two mules. The judge decided that the two eight-year-old mules named Sam and John were the property of Hall and White's client, ordering the man who filed the lawsuit to return the mules or pay their client $500 for them. The man continued to insist that those were his mules and was granted an appeal by the judge.[5]

White had come full circle — from her rural childhood in a farming community to the halls of government in the nation's capital and back again — honing her legal skills and helping her community as a country lawyer.

CHAPTER 7

Determined to Foment a Rebellion

Sue White was an avid reader and contributed book reviews to a Nashville newspaper. She was not afraid to tackle controversial books and subjects. She gleaned lessons from the biographies of great women in history.

In 1929 White reviewed the book *Man and Woman: A Study of Secondary and Tertiary Sexual Characteristics* by Havelock Ellis, first published in 1894 and revised in 1929. Ellis was an English physician who studied human sexuality. In 1897 he co-authored the first medical textbook in English on homosexuality. He also published on sexual practices and transgender psychology.

"In many chapters it is technical enough to require the frequent use of a dictionary, but it never fails to be interesting," White wrote, concluding:

Havelock Ellis has no patience with any assumption of superiority on

the part of either sex. For instance, he points out that against the greater
genius of man must be set off the greater idiocy of man—or words to that
effect; and that women strike the happy medium between these
variational tendencies toward genius and idiocy as enjoyed by mere man.
The fair sex may thank him or not for his kind words. . .It is small
comfort to be ruled out of the genius class almost altogether, but if this is
what science is to do for women, it will no doubt please them somewhat
to know that they belong to the middling class of dumbbells rather than
just plain idiots.[1]

In an April 1929 review of the book *Abigail Adams*, White
expressed her admiration for Adams. She marveled that while
John Adams was in Philadelphia founding a nation, Abigail ran
the farm, tutored her children, nursed the sick among her relatives
and their servants, opened her home for refugees from
beleaguered Boston, attended township meetings, visited the
camps, kept an eye on "prices and politics, neighbors and
enemies," and reported on it all to John in letters "full of
tenderness and good hard common sense."

White speculated that Abigail Adams was being prophetic
when Adams said in 1776, "If particular care and attention is not
paid to the ladies, we are determined to foment a rebellion, and
will not hold ourselves bound by any laws in which we have no

voice or representation." White said Adams showed her independence early on by marrying John Adams over the protests of her family, who thought she could do better than marrying a farmer and a lawyer.

White responded to criticism that the book was idealistic — that the Abigail Adams described by the book's author was too good to be true. White disagreed. "Without doubt she was not frail. She had a head of her own and used it. . .This biography is to be welcomed by those who have long deplored the grudging slowness of the recognition accorded the mothers of the republic."[2]

White wrote a January 1929 review of the biography *The Terrible Siren: Victoria Woodhull,* published in 1928. Woodhull was a leader of the U.S. suffrage movement in the late 1800s and considered by some to be the first woman to run for President of the United States, which she did in 1872 as the Equal Rights candidate. White praised the book as "the amazing tale of an amazing woman" and called Woodhull "magnificent in her contradictions. . .There were few minor acts in her life. All that she did was with a bang."[3] It was an apt description for Woodhull and White herself.

In a May 1928 review of the book *The Family in the Making*, White wrote, "A cheerful feminism runs through this historical study of the family as an institution." She noted that the book's author predicted that the family unit will weather the present storms and not disintegrate as current pundits predict. "But there will be no return to the old order," she wrote, adding that the family's "salvation will be liberated woman, playing her part as a woman rather than as an imitator of man."[4]

CHAPTER 8

Lady Warrior

White was frustrated with the old-boy network of Southern politics. She vented her anger in a fuming letter to fellow suffragist and Democrat Mary Dewson in November 1928:

Women have been discouraged by the rank and file of the party organization to take part in party activities. We still have the old anti-suffrage attitude in the South. Women have been indifferent and their indifference has been preached to them, aided, abetted, and encouraged. They have viewed politics as something they should stay away from. They have been told so and have believed it and the few feminists who have tried to push in have been slapped in the face. (I am talking about the South now.) And the few women who have been artificially reared up as leaders are not leaders of women and have been reared not to lead women but to fool them.

White was angry that preachers and "artificially reared women leaders" were fooling women into believing that politics would ruin women's traditional roles in the home and church.

White encouraged the Democratic Party to launch an educational campaign among voters — men and women — to reverse the anti-suffrage attitudes in the South. She said it would be a bitter pill for the "old boys" of the Southern Democratic Party, but "the eastern and western leaders can make them swallow it."[1]

After the defeat of Democrat Al Smith in the 1928 presidential election, there was an urgent need to rebuild the Democratic Party. White joined former Wyoming governor Nellie Tayloe Ross, now vice chairman of the Democratic National Committee (DNC), to organize women across the country for the party.

Ross admired White for her thought-provoking questions. "She was forever wanting to get ahead faster," Ross wrote. "She was loyal to her friends, her party, her state and her country. She would sacrifice herself, but not her friends or her principles. . .She was a superior organizer, generating ideas, enlisting people, stimulating interest. She could instill strength into a reed."[2]

While battling the antiquated attitudes of the Southern traditionalists, White found a home in the more progressive environment of the nation's capital. Her neighbors at the Cecil Apartments in Washington, D.C. were diverse in their nationalities, professions and partnerships. She had Czech, German and Spanish neighbors. They included a physician, an advertising agent, a lawyer, a librarian, a teacher, a surgeon, and a government physicist. Six apartments were occupied by same-sex partners.[3]

White left her job as executive secretary with the DNC in December 1933.[4] She resigned in November, but party leaders persuaded her to stay on until the end of year, since she was one of the best informed and most popular women in the party. Earlier that year, First Lady Eleanor Roosevelt had recruited White, Ross and Dewson to help her review applications from women for federal appointments in President Roosevelt's new administration and to make hiring recommendations. "Mrs. Roosevelt thinks that our recommendations will be treated with respect," Ross wrote.[5]

White next joined the federal National Recovery Administration (NRA) recently established by President Roosevelt. The intent of the NRA was to promote fair competition in the wake of the Depression. The public enthusiastically supported the program at the start, but later turned against it. The Supreme Court declared the National Recovery Act unconstitutional in 1935. The NRA was dismantled, and White's job was eliminated.[6] Before she left, White tried to salvage the knowledge and experience gained from the program by protecting the records and compiling the final reports.[7]

White's friends suggested that she join the new Social Security Board, which they predicted would grow into an important agency. The idea appealed to White. The board's goal to relieve the suffering of those in need mirrored her own beliefs. Dewson and Eleanor Roosevelt talked with an influential member of the Social Security Board about a job for White, and she joined its first legal staff in early 1936.[8]

The general counsel for the Social Security Board was Jack B. Tate. Tate grew up just a few miles from White in rural West Tennessee. They first met when Tate was a young boy and White a young woman. In letters to her Tennessee friends, White said it was a pleasure working in Washington for "little Jack Tate."

Years later Tate recalled how radical and controversial the new Social Security program was considered when it began. Opponents of Social Security claimed that U.S. citizens would have to wear dog tags — allegations started by publishing magnate William Randolph Hearst in his newspapers during the 1936 presidential campaign. Hearst was opposed to the New Deal and a foe of President Roosevelt.

Tate called White a rarity — both a Southern gentlewoman and a lady warrior. He admired her sense of humor and "delicious sense of the ridiculous." He said her political skills were so effective that she "delighted the wise and distressed the stupid."

Tate was especially proud that White had mastered the "fast vanishing art of the blood-curdling Rebel Yell."[9]

Fellow attorney Rosalie Moynahan met White in 1937 after she joined the Social Security administration. Moynahan had been in private practice in New York City. She was dismayed when told that she would share an office with another attorney — Miss Sue White of Tennessee. Moynahan remembered White upon their first meeting as "dark and vivid; her hair beginning to gray; deep-set, merry eyes; with a sharp wit and naturally caustic tongue softened by understanding of men and women."

Moynahan later learned that White had the same reluctance to share an office, saying they both believed in the principle of "one lawyer-one office." But they quickly bonded and remained friends.[10]

White's wit, sarcasm and outsized sense of humor were hallmarks of her personality. But she wasn't limited to sharp retorts. She worked to be a respected orator for her causes.

In 1941 she took a public speaking course in Washington taught by Mrs. Hugh Butler, a speech teacher and wife of a U.S. diplomat. Butler had based the *Capital Speakers* course on her studies with an English parliamentary coach while living in London. The classes were attended by members of Congress, foreign diplomats, and professional women. White received a *Superior* grade of 94 for the course. In her notes, which she titled *Important Things*, White reminded herself to practice breath control, relax her throat, and avoid mumbling.[11] She had a passion to be heard and was willing to work for it.

CHAPTER 9

World at War

White's older sister Lucy was a San Francisco newspaper reporter when she married German music director and teacher Frederick Schiller in January 1916. Schiller previously directed in Munich and Nuremberg, Germany. The couple stayed in San Francisco after they married.[1]

The next year, in April 1917, the United States declared war on Germany and joined its allies in World War I.

Six months later White oversaw the drive to register Tennessee women for war service on the home front. The registration drive was led by the Council of National Defense. White sent a letter to the county chairmen of the registration drive, warning of efforts by "German sympathizers and propagandists" to keep women from registering. She contended that women were being told that if they signed the registration card the government would confiscate their canned food and send it to the soldiers. Other women thought that they would be sent away from their home and children and made to work for free. Others were falsely convinced that the registration drive was a suffrage movement in disguise. White wrote to the county leaders:

Let us see that no loyal American woman is misled by such efforts of German sympathizers who make insidious appeals to prejudice and ignorance. One of the boldest attempts of these propagandists has been to try to make it appear that this registration of women is entirely a suffrage movement. . .They who deliberately seek to keep a woman from responding to the call of her country upon such a specious argument are lining themselves up with the enemies of our country.

White convinced the Tennessee governor and National Defense Council to extend the deadline for registration for two extra weeks to allow Tennessee women more time to register. The extension worked, and 75,000 women were registered to help the war effort at home.[2]

During World War I, White's younger brother Marshall was a sergeant with the Second Army 23rd Engineers, stationed in France. Marshall was one of 5,000 engineers recruited by the U.S. Army in just three months. He left for France in March 1918. Marshall wrote to his sister from the front lines in July:[3]

At the same old place, July 28, 1918

Dearest Susan:

Yesterday just as I was about to get the men out for inspection the mail clerk brought me a letter each from you and Lucy, both of which I read very hurriedly and then must have eaten — for I have looked high and low for them and have been unable to find hair or hide.

You ask if the river valleys are the same here as they are in America — really for definite and generally application on this subject I must refer you to any first class atlas. The particular valley where I am is very broad and flat with vast expanses of meadow which at sometimes must be marshy. The river in reality is a bay with several feet of tide, which runs up into every little ditch and canal, of which there are quite a number. The floor of the valley is only a foot or two above extreme high tide. On the sides of this valley floor are gently undulating hills — even Madison County could furnish more imposing ones. But though all the hills are very low they seem to furnish a surprising number of quiet vistas. This camp is very well located, and has a very good view of the harbor. My work is such that I am busy early in the morning and late at night, but quite often am able to steal off in the middle of the afternoon for a walk along the charming lanes. Do you remember the "Queen Anne's Lace" that used to grow out around Highland Park? It grows here in the fallow fields and the blackberries in the roadside hedge are just getting ripe. If I had on a Sam Browne belt, dignity would forbid my picking these — that is philosophy. I am beginning to evolve myself a new philosophy — only I am afraid that it will prove to be a gambler's — army life certainly gives a strong impression of the omnipotence of Chance.

Perhaps very fortunately for you I was interrupted sparing you an impromptu discourse on the Wiles of Fortune. A new sergeant came to the detachment a few days ago, one whom I had never known before. As I was a little curious about his personality, I agreed to go out "buvetting" with him. I found that in civil life he had been a travelling automobile salesman and was, is and always will be a bore, world without end, amen

Lots of love, Marshall

White did not reply to his letter, much to her brother's frustration. He wrote her again in October.[4]

France, Oct 13th, 1918

Dear Sue:

This one-sided correspondence I have been attempting to keep up with you is I fear not a huge success as there is probably very little in my letters of interest and I do not get any from you at all. Have not heard from you since I left the base post and that has been two <u>long</u> months. I have seen a good deal since then — some things that I can not and some *that I do not care to tell. I had a touch of something like ptomaine poisoning and was pretty sick for three days but am getting on my feet again.*

We can hear all kinds of peace rumors, but do not put a great deal of credence in them as long as the big guns are making such an infernal racket all around us. At any rate we do not want peace until we can have one which we can feel assured will be a <u>lasting</u> one.

It's a drizzly cold day and I am trying to keep the fire going with green wood. I am in an ugly mood I fear. Hoping not to impart any of the same.

Marshall

Weeks later, on November 11, 1918, the Armistice treaty was signed. The long global nightmare of World War I finally ended.

SOME WOMAN HAD TO FIGHT

The 23rd Engineers returned home in May 1919. But this would not be the only world war to impact White and her family.

During World War II, the federal government ordered the forced relocation and incarceration of 112,000 Japanese Americans living on the West Coast. They were given only a few days to dispose of their property and gather the belongings they could carry with them. Their fellow citizens and neighbors took advantage of this injustice and bought their possessions and properties at a fraction of their worth.[5]

Lucy was living in the Richmond District of San Francisco, near the Presidio. Lucy wrote to her sister in April 1942:[6]

Dear Sue:

I haven't heard from you since just after Xmas, except for the note you enclosed to Marshall with the birth statements, which he forwarded to me with them.

I would like to hear the news from you however. Things are just the same with us except that one of F's choral clubs will probably stop rehearsing weekly, and meet only monthly, on account of the fact that war conditions make it impossible for all the members to attend rehearsals. This may mean only a small reduction of our income, and it may be the beginning of the end of it. We don't know. We can't find a farm that promises anything, or haven't so far. We are even going to look at some of the places that the Jap farmers are being evacuated from, but there is not much hope there as most of their farms were "stoop" farms, vegetables, berries, etc.—too strenuous for our old bones. I don't feel the least bit worried, so don't you. If we find anything we think worth trying to get we will write or wire you. Meanwhile we dug up our lawn and took out some of the smaller shrubs in the rear and made us a Victory garden or at least a Vegetable garden, about 36 by 15 feet.

Americans were encouraged during the war to grow "victory gardens" to feed themselves so that other agricultural produce would be available to feed the troops. Lucy described growing onions, radishes, beets, Swiss chard, spinach, beans, celery, tomatoes, cauliflower, lettuce, cabbage and strawberries to feed her and her husband.

Like others living on the West Coast, in fear of air attacks from Japan, she had prepared to defend her home:

I have my bathtub full of water, and buckets of sand on each floor, and am getting one for the roof next week. Have a 50 foot garden hose attached (or to be attached) to the cold water faucet in hand basin of the bathroom, and a strong cord attached to the roof to pull it up. Also an old bucket spray we used on the orchard trees down the peninsula, which we have resurrected and rejuvenated. Also two shovels and two axes, and as I am here alone until 12 or 1, I shall certainly have all the tools to fight incendiaries when they come—as many as I can handle anyway.

Please let me have a note from you.

Lovingly, Lucy

A gossip-filled 1943 letter to White from a friend in Tennessee reveals the anti-Semitic attitudes that pervaded the United States at the same time the horrors of the concentration camps were being inflicted in Europe. Her friend wrote of the "Jerusalem invasion" of a local neighborhood, explaining how the local society ladies fawn over the Jewish owner of the department store to get a discount price, but now are upset that the Jewish owner has bought a house in their neighborhood and will be "right under foot." She told White that a local businessman bought a home in the same neighborhood "to keep it from being sold to another Jew."

The friend neither defended nor decried the society ladies for their anti-Semitic views, but she was eager to keep White abreast of the local gossip, solicited or not by White. The friend concluded wistfully, "I am hoping for an early peace but not expecting it."[7]

It would be two more harrowing years before World War II ended and the concentration camps were liberated.

CHAPTER 10

Finding Home

To her friends, White seemed happiest in the last years of her life. She was openly disturbed by the global rise of totalitarianism, but the home she shared in Alexandria, Virginia with her partner Armstrong was a warm and welcoming place for their friends to gather.[1]

Their next-door neighbor Elizabeth Spence would marvel at White and Armstrong outside wielding hammers and hoes as they screened in their back porch, paved the terrace, planted a garden, and built a brick wall around the flower beds. Spence recalled, "I was astounded and impressed by their energy and daring, for they were some years older than I and it was long before the advent of the do-it-yourself crazes had put hammers in the hands of women. Sue's skill in carpentry never ceased to amaze me, and I found it hard to believe that a busy government attorney would have the energy, time and know-how to construct shelves and bookcases from odds and ends of wood as she did."[2]

White's carpentry skills were forged as a child in the rural South, working alongside her brother. She was an orphan by 13, learning to fend for herself in a man's world. The caricature of a genteel Southern belle had no connection to White's life.

Spence said she would chat with White across the imaginary line that separated their backyards and remembered how she enjoyed White's quick wit and hearty laughter.

Armstrong recalled the first time she saw White was in 1934 at a Washington party. She noticed that White was "tall, stately, and impressive. She had the largest, most luminous, most expressive dark brown eyes I ever saw, and she possessed a beautiful, rich, melodious voice. . .I asked who she was and was informed: 'That's Sue White; she's very powerful in the Democratic party.' We were introduced and said a few words."

At the time, White was serving as assistant to Mary Rumsey, chairman of the Consumers Advisory Board of the National Recovery Administration. Later Armstrong was appointed as a consultant to the Consumers Advisory Board, where she met White a second time.

About the time that Armstrong joined, Rumsey was injured in a hunting accident and died a month later. White and Rumsey were close, and White was grief stricken by her death. There was confusion over how to manage the consumer board with their leader gone, and White turned to economist Armstrong for advice. Armstrong was known for her work on the economics of consumption.

Like White had done in 1936, Armstrong joined the Social Security Administration in 1937 as a social economist in the Bureau of Research and Statistics. There White and Armstrong were able to continue their professional collaboration.

Armstrong wanted to move out of the city in 1937 to avoid the stifling heat of another Washington summer. White owned a rental house in Arlington, Virginia. At first, White proposed that she and Armstrong move there. Instead, they decided to jointly purchase a new house in Alexandria that was more convenient. Armstrong, her mother and White moved together to the new house.[3]

After years of transition and tumult, White finally was home.

CHAPTER 11

The Final Battle

White had been struggling with poor health long before her friends and family were aware. She kept a small notepad in 1937 and 1938 of the medicines she was taking — gall bladder pills, a phenobarbital sedative, a codeine opioid pain reliever, and multiple laxatives.[1] Armstrong later wrote:

Despite her remarkable energy, I think Sue was not well all the years I knew her; she went rather often to doctors for relief, especially to a doctor of Osteopathy who was able to help her. After her final illness struck her down and surgery was undertaken, the surgeon instructed her friends never to let her know she was afflicted with cancer, and we never did, nor did she ever mention it. She spoke frequently of going back to work "soon" and once said she believed she would arrange to have a cot placed in her office so that she could go to work but have a chance to rest when she got tired.[2]

White's Washington and Tennessee friends stayed in touch

during her illness. From the Treasury Department in June 1942, her friend Edness Kimball Wilkins wrote, "Florence says you have had fine results from the blood transfusions. am so glad you are feeling stronger. I'll get out to see you soon."[3]

In August 1942 White was a patient at Garfield Hospital in Washington. A letter arrived from her gossip-loving friend in Tennessee. She informed White that one neighborhood was running after the new wartime millionaires made rich by ammunition production, that a prominent citizen's second wife had taken a lover, and that a local woman was seen driving the chief of police around in her car. "We need you to straighten us out," she implored, hoping to instill the strength in White to return to Tennessee for the sake of her friends.[4]

Another letter was hand delivered to White at Garfield Hospital. Its return address was simply *The White House*. Accompanied by flowers, it was a personal note from Eleanor Roosevelt, expressing Roosevelt's hope that White would be out of the hospital soon.[5]

White also received get-well wishes from friend and global peace activist Mabel Vernon:[6]

Suzie dear:

I am so sorry you are laid up. Get well soon—I have to stop another war—a bigger and better one—I need you.

Love, Mabel

Armstrong kept White's sister Lucy in San Francisco updated on White's illness. In May 1942 Lucy wrote back to Armstrong:[7]

I am glad to know Sue is better, but wish she were much better still. It all doesn't sound so good to me. Marshall says it isn't as though it was anything from which Sue will not recover. I sometimes almost wish I was a man, when I see the ease with which they can deny to themselves any disturbing fact, however apparent.

Of course he might have been only trying to "build up" my "morale." Of course she must stay in the hospital until she is enough recovered for them to find out what caused this trouble, and try to cure it. I wonder if it could have been due to some intestinal or rectal ulcer, old and unknown.

What comforted me most of all was to know that Sue's friends have been so attentive to her. There is so little I can do from this distance, and that hurts. If it is considered advisable, after Sue has recovered enough to be dismissed from the hospital, I could perhaps come and get her and bring her home with me, if she will come. I think she enjoys Washington and her work, and it will be hard for her to give them up, or to admit it is necessary for her to give them up. I think such a suggestion at this time might be so discouraging to her as to be hurtful.

Please tell Sue the feeling out here is that the danger of Jap incendiaries is very very little now. (In case she ever seems to fear anything for us on that score.) And Frederick's business so far has suffered no ill consequences of the war. I think we have fared that way better than most people. Like every one else we have more expenses, taxes, etc., than before, but by economy we get by very well so far. (This in case she shows any worry on that score.)

Thank you so much for your careful good letters. They told me just the things I wanted to know about. And thank you for your attention to Sue and her affairs.

Very sincerely, Lucy White Schiller

In September 1942, Marshall also wrote to his sister and Armstrong.[8] He was happy that White had improved enough to leave the hospital, but he was worried that she would not have enough fuel to heat her home during the cold Washington winter due to wartime shortages.

Marshall said that he had seen a demonstration of a newly invented kitchen appliance — a liquefier — and thought this device may be useful for White to maintain her nutrition during her illness. Unknown to him, Marshall was describing the first smoothies, introduced into the American diet in the 1940s by the Waring Blender company. He wrote:

It occurred to me that it might help in feeding Sue. In two or three minutes, it makes a liquid of all vegetables (raw), including carrots, apples, liver, beef, etc. I have seen it work; you have to start with tomato juice, fruit juice, milk or other liquid, then slice in your solid vegetable, and turn on the current for a minute or so. The product is a smooth liquid without any solid particles that you can feel with your tongue. It will handle anything except woody seed, such as grape seed, orange seed, etc. If you think it would be of any use to you at all, I will get one and send it immediately. I called up my friend tonight to ask about it, he asked that I come for a demonstration. I went and found him and his wife to be quite a food fadist, but it is really an efficient machine.

I had intended writing a longer letter, but am frankly all tired out from hearing a talk all evening of what should or should not be eaten. I notice too, that this typewriter does not spell very well tonight, it's that way sometimes when it gets tired.

Let me know what you think of the Liquefier, if you think you could use one, I will send one.

Best love to both of you, Marshall

In the 1930s White was a regular visitor to the home of close friend and fellow suffragist Betty Gram Swing. White would entertain Swing's three children with stories of her childhood in the South.

Swing kept a photo of White displayed in her home, among the photos of her children and grandchildren. Swing loved White's "whimsical look, half wise and half pixie. . .The hair is short and over-the-brow bangs frame the kindest eyes I have ever seen."[9]

Like White, Swing was a former suffragist prisoner. Swing first met White during the White House protests, but they bonded during the Nineteenth Amendment ratification campaign. Swing affectionately referred to the pair as "old campaigners and jail birds like ourselves."

They last saw each other a few days before White's death. Swing read to White at her bedside the poems of British poet and Jesuit priest Gerard Manly Hopkins. Weakened by her terminal illness, White tried to console Swing, "You know I am going back to work on Monday. I am alright and you must not worry."

Armstrong wrote of her admiration for White's determination and the kindness of their friends during her illness:

No more gallant patient ever lived. As long as she could sit up, she kept busy with music, painting, reading and crocheting. Her friends cheered her with attentions; a man in her office even made her a gift of some fireplace coal which he was able through connections to obtain and so helped keep her warm when the rigors of wartime rationing skimped too much our supply of fuel oil for adequate heating.

She gave people a lift, even during her last months when she was growing weaker day by day.

In her time, White was affectionately called Miss Sue and sometimes Lady Warrior. She never shrank from a fight, even as a patient. After a hard-fought battle with cancer, White died quietly at her home on May 6, 1943 "after her beloved azaleas came into full bloom."[10]

She was 55. Her devoted partner Armstrong was by her side.

CHAPTER 12

Whatever the Cost

Throughout her life, White had a vision for a fair and equal America.

In 1920, as research chairman of the National Woman's Party, White worked with women lawyers across the country to examine state laws for inequalities and discrimination against women.

White was not pleased with what she found: A married woman may own property, but in some states the husband controlled it. In states without community property laws, the property that resulted from the joint labor of husband and wife belonged to the husband. In some states, a father could designate custody of his children in his will to someone other than the mother upon his death. In every state, the husband got to choose the domicile and the wife must live in the place he selects, or be found guilty of desertion, even though she may be the one supporting the family financially. An American woman lost her citizenship and right to vote if she married a man of another nationality. Women also were not on equal footing in the federal and state civil service systems for appointments and salaries.

White proposed changes to federal and state laws, making women eligible to civil offices on the same terms and conditions as men. She proposed a state law repealing the common law principle that a wife's identity is merged with that of her husband; a marriage law requiring joint decisions about residence and control of children; and repeal of the federal statute depriving American women who marry foreigners of their U.S. citizenship.[1]

In 1923 White helped draft the Lucretia Mott Amendment, the precursor to the Equal Rights Amendment: *Men and women shall have equal rights throughout the United States and every place subject to its jurisdiction.*

Several lawyers in the National Woman's Party drafted and announced the proposed amendment to the U.S. Constitution at the Seneca Falls women's rights conference in 1923. Armstrong wrote of White in 1959, "She was always very proud of this effort, though of course disappointed in the way its passage has lagged."[2] The same is still true today.

The state convention of the Tennessee Business and Professional Women's Clubs met in June 1927. Justice Florence E. Allen of the Ohio Supreme Court, the first woman Supreme Court jurist in the United States, spoke at the convention, encouraging more Tennessee women to become lawyers.[3]

At the conference, White introduced a resolution stating that this group of Tennessee businesswomen opposed all laws that bar women from employment on the grounds of marriage. Her vision did not come to fruition until 1964, with the passage of the Civil Rights Act.

White had the foresight to imagine the practical benefits of men and women breaking from their traditional gender roles to pursue their strengths. In a review of the 1929 book *Marriage in the Modern Manner*, she wrote:

If a woman finds that she has a natural bent for playing the stock market and none at all for playing the piano, her energies are no longer limited to bad piano playing. . .In the fifty-fifty marriage, if a man happens to be a better cook than the wife, why shouldn't he cook the dinner? If she is a better businessman (say the authors) and he a better home maker, it might even be more sensible for him to remain at home and keep house and let her support the family than to reverse the positions.

Traditional speaking, this sounds terrible, but to face the terrible is to be brave, and the book suggests that the husband who has faced this situation and agreed with his wife to divide their life work according to the abilities, time and strength of each, is the real master of his fate rather than the slave to outward traditions.[4]

During the campaign for the vote, suffragists had harnessed the power of publicity, through parades, protests and pageants. The pageants were performance art with a political message. They were designed to motivate volunteers, generate headlines, raise money and recruit new supporters.

Hazel MacKaye was the best-known pageant director. She created four pageants for the Congressional Union for Woman Suffrage and National Woman's Party between 1913 and 1923. The first pageant, *The Allegory,* was held March 1913 in Washington, D.C. Alice Paul  received permission to use the grand steps of the Treasury Building during working hours to stage the performance. It featured 100 women and children dressed in costumes of ancient Greece, representing the ideals Freedom, Justice, Peace, Charity, Liberty and Hope. More than 20,000 people watched.

MacKaye's final pageant for the NWP — the Equal Rights pageant — was held in September 1923 in Colorado Springs, Colorado. It celebrated the 75th anniversary of the first women's rights convention, in 1848 in Seneca Falls, New York.[5]

The goal was to attract new members as the NWP prepared to have the Equal Rights Amendment introduced in Congress. The pageant was staged at the Garden of the Gods, the majestic sandstone rock formations set against the grandeur of 14,000-foot Pikes Peak.

The women dressed in costumes from the 1840s, an homage to their early suffragist sisters. The pageant rivaled the spectacle of that first performance on the steps of the Treasury Building.

White was the principal speaker that day. She memorialized the sacrifices of those who went before her and the sustained, uphill climb to equality:

Truth speaks with the same authority as generations come and go. Seventy-five years ago women of a day that is gone arose to salute the truth calling within their souls. Another generation has followed and another still, proud to affirm the right proclaimed by those who pioneered. Here we see today, not merely the women of yesterday. We see a brave allegiance to an idea as young and fresh as it has ever been. It never can grow old. It has the vitality of life itself. It speaks the authority of truth.

Here in the fresh free air, in the lea of the mountain side, the sky above, the green earth beneath and mighty rocks for a background, abides the spirit of freedom. An elemental idea in an elemental setting. This is our temple and we come with reverence, remembering the deeds of those who had the vision and followed it. No one living today, man or woman, but has been benefited by the pioneer women whom we honor here. Each of us here today owes the women of 1848 deep gratitude for bringing their cause to the great, new fearless west, where pioneer met pioneer, together in faith and courage.

As in the days following 1848, the west proved the most fertile ground for the enfranchisement of women, so will it lead the way in carrying out the full program of equal rights, inaugurated at that time. In July of this year, at Seneca Falls, the National Woman's party voted to introduce into Congress the Lucretia Mott amendment, demanding that men and women shall have equal rights in the United States and every place subject to its jurisdiction. In many states laws are such that the husband owns his wife's earnings, controls her property, fixes her legal residence, has the superior rights to the care and custody of the child, and in various ways exercises dominion over her. Young women find themselves barred from educational institutions supported by public funds, and girls attempting to enter the professions find obstacles that their brothers do not find. Such a condition cannot, must not, continue. It is inevitable that women shall take not only their lives into their own hands, but that they shall share equally the responsibility of the lives that they ordain as the mothers of the race.

We have paused to trace the path of the early beginning, to test and to know the ground on which we stand, and now we face the climb ahead. If the Woman's party program is carried out—and it will be carried out— not one of these girls among all these little ones will meet that curious, complex frustration of effort that other women have met in the attempt to be merely themselves.

We have commemorated the first equal rights meeting that began 75 years ago. We cannot be content to memorialize and leave the work then begun unfinished. No higher honor can be paid a prophet than to make the vision come true. In this everyone here can help by giving support to the campaign of the National Woman's party. How much do you value that which has been accomplished for women in the past 75 years? How precious to your little daughter is the heritage that is hers? How much do you desire that the yolk shall be entirely lifted? Women must be freed of their subjection whatever the cost. What you can give here today will measure the length of the next step to be taken and register your individual response to the appeal of women for unhampered lives.[6]

White's brief, eloquent speech — her Gettysburg Address — was credited for the success of that final pageant and marked the start of a new era in the women's rights movement.

EPILOGUE
Gaiety and Grief

Over the years White was encouraged by her friends to write a memoir of her life and the people she had met. She always declined, saying the truth would hurt too many people and, if she did not tell the truth, what would be the value of it.[1]

But in a 1929 book review, White wrote her prescription for a first-rate biography. She said it must be a vast and painstaking labor. She insisted that a good biography must not be dry bones, but a portrait of a vivid and intelligent life, filled with gaiety and grief.[2]

Sue Shelton White lived that vivid life – in broad, sweeping strokes and brash, bold colors. These pages have sought to tell her complicated, audacious and inspiring truth.

She brought it all to the fight, punching a path forward for women. Today a new generation picks up the gloves and steps in the ring — to fight on for equal justice for all.

Acknowledgements

Thank you to research librarians Jack Wood and Evelyn Keele, for sharing their knowledge and resources to uncover the historical treasures of the Tennessee Room at the Jackson-Madison County Library.

Thank you to the Madison County Archives for preserving and protecting vital historical records and to archivist Lorri Skelton for her expertise and shared enthusiasm while we pored over the musty pages of court records from almost 100 years ago.

Most of all, thank you to my husband Will for his talent and support during my two-year quest to tell the story of Sue Shelton White.

Notes

Chapter 1: Rowdyism about to Break Loose

[1]"Denmark Marks 100 Years of Women's Right to Vote," *The Local*, June 4, 2015.

[2]"Iceland Celebrates Women's Rights Day," *Iceland Monitor*, June 19, 2016.

[3]Affidavit of Birth, February 1942, Sue Shelton White Papers, Schlesinger Library, Radcliffe Institute, Harvard University.

[4]"Mrs. Dudley Named as Suffrage Leader," *Nashville Tennessean*, October 9, 1915.

[5]"Woman's Party Leaders Coming: Will Speak in Defense of Their Methods," *Nashville Tennessean*, November 16, 1917

[6]Rebecca Hourwich Reyher to Florence Armstrong, September 26, 1958, Sue Shelton White Papers, Schlesinger Library.

[7]"Urge That Suffrage Speaker Be Heard: Citizens' Meeting in Jackson Commends Miss Younger to Nashville Mayor," *Nashville Tennessean*, November 23, 1917.

[8]Reyher to Armstrong, September 26, 1958, Sue Shelton White Papers, Schlesinger Library.

[9]Sue White to Sen. Kenneth McKellar, June 23, 1925, Sue Shelton White Papers, Schlesinger Library.

[10]Reyher to Armstrong, September 26, 1958, Sue Shelton White Papers, Schlesinger Library.

Chapter 2: Every Mother's Daughter

[1]"Democrats! Take Notice," *Nashville Tennessean*, November 23, 1917.

[2]"Picketing White House," *Nashville Tennessean*, November 23, 1917.

[3]"Suffragists Burn Wilson in Effigy; Sue White Leader," *Nashville Tennessean*, February 10, 1919.

[4]Doris Stevens, *Jailed for Freedom: The Story of the Militant American Suffragist Movement* (New York: Boni and Liveright, 1920), p. 361.

[5]"The female nuisances," *Lexington Progress*, November 23, 1917.

[6]"Suffragists Loyal," *Nashville Tennessean*, November 24, 1917.

[7]"Suffrage Prisoners," *American Memory*, Library of Congress.

[8]"Prison Special on Way—Our Sue Aboard," *Nashville Tennessean*, February 17, 1919.

[9]"Suffrage Bill is Passed by Bare Majority, Senator Wikle Casts Deciding Vote Against His Best Judgment," *Nashville Tennessean*, April 15, 1919.

[10]*United States Census* for Washington, D.C., 1920.

[11]Florence A. Armstrong, "Sue Shelton White (1887-1943)," February 1959, Sue Shelton White Papers, Schlesinger Library.

[12]"Miss Sue S. White, Suffrage Leader, Headed Woman's Party Fight in Tennessee for the 19th Amendment--Dies at 55, Burned Wilson in Effigy," *New York Times*, May 8, 1943.

[13]"Plan to Send Women to Congress Pushed, Miss Sue White Coming to Tennessee to Work Toward That End," *Nashville Tennessean*, July 22, 1925.

Chapter 3: Some Woman Had to Fight

[1]"Unanimous Election of Miss Sue White," *Nashville Tennessean*, December 23, 1917.

[2]"Market Sought for Brooms Made by Blind," *Nashville Tennessean*, November 18, 1918.

[3]"Woman Leader Really Likes Steady Fight," *Elmira, NY Telegram*, September 21, 1934, Sue Shelton White Papers, Schlesinger Library.

[4]"Consumers' Council Organizer Can't Stay Out of 'Good' Fight," *Torrington Register*, September 21, 1934.

[5]Susan Ware, *Beyond Suffrage: Women in the New Deal* (Cambridge: Harvard University Press, 1981), p. 95-96.

[6]Armstrong, "Sue Shelton White (1887-1943)," Sue Shelton White Papers, Schlesinger Library.

[7]Florence Brewer Boeckel, *Equal Rights,* July-August 1943 issue, Sue Shelton White Papers, Schlesinger Library.

[8]"Social News and Activities of Women's Clubs," *Nashville Tennessean*, August 27, 1933.

[9]"First Decade 1917-1927: Establishing Traditions and Blazing Trails," *Looking Back, Moving Forward*, Women's Bar Association of the District of Columbia, May 17, 2017, p. 48.

[10]"Illustrious Career Ended with Burial in Oakdale Cemetery Here Sunday," *Marysville Journal-Tribune*, February 27, 1939.

[11]Armstrong, "Sue Shelton White (1887-1943)," Sue Shelton White Papers, Schlesinger Library.

Chapter 4: Not Such a White Elephant

[1]"Miss White Becomes M'Kellar's Secretary," *Nashville Tennessean*, December 17, 1920.

[2]"Order Admitting Attorney to Practice Law," Clerk of Circuit Court of Madison County, August 4, 1923, Sue Shelton White Papers, Schlesinger Library.

[3]"The Lee Family," *The New England Historical and Genealogical Register*, p. 215.

[4]Sue White to Sen. Kenneth McKellar, June 23, 1925, Sue Shelton White Papers, Schlesinger Library.

[5]Sen. Kenneth McKellar to Sue White, June 25, 1925, Sue Shelton White Papers, Schlesinger Library.

[6]Clive Giboire, *Lovingly, Georgia: The Complete Correspondence of Georgia O'Keefe and Anita Pollitzer* (New York: Simon & Schuster, 1990)

[7]Anita Pollitzer to Mrs. Isaac Reese, December 1925, Sue Shelton White Papers, Schlesinger Library.

[8]Anita Pollitzer to Mrs. John M. Kenny, December 1925, Sue Shelton White Papers, Schlesinger Library.

[9]Sen. Kenneth McKellar to Sue White, July 6, 1926, Sue Shelton White Papers, Schlesinger Library.

[10]Sue White to Sen. Kenneth McKellar, July 8, 1926, Sue Shelton White Papers, Schlesinger Library

[11]Sen. Kenneth McKellar to Sue White, July 14, 1926, Sue Shelton White Papers, Schlesinger Library.

[12]Sen. Kenneth McKellar to Sue White, July 19, 1926, Sue Shelton White Papers, Schlesinger Library.

[13]"By the Way," *Nashville Tennessean*, November 28, 1926.

Chapter 5: A Full Partnership without Embarrassment

[1]"Order Admitting Attorney to Practice Law," Sue Shelton White Papers, Schlesinger Library.

[2]Armstrong, "Sue Shelton White (1887-1943)," Sue Shelton White Papers, Schlesinger Library.

[3]Nellie Tayloe Ross, "Comments on Sue White," September 23, 1958, Sue Shelton White Papers, Schlesinger Library.

[4]Sue White to Hu C. Anderson, July 22, 1926, Sue Shelton White Papers, Schlesinger Library.

[5]Annie Lee Cavness Hill v C.W. Hill, *Minutes of Chancery Court of Madison County*, January 27, 1928, pp. 531-532.

[6]C.A. Tomlinson v J.S. Eubanks, *Minutes of Chancery Court of Madison County*, September 22, 1927, pp. 444-445.

[7]Madison County for the use of Drainage District No. 4 et al v Glopus Manley et al, *Minutes of Chancery Court of Madison County*, January 6, 1930, pp 506-508.

[8]Mrs. Olliver Snipes v Sam C. Hagy, Henry Colby, Delco Light Company and General Motors Acceptance Corporation, *Rule Docket of Chancery Court of Madison County*, pp. 145-146.

[9]Sam Moore, "The Delco-Light Plant," *Farm Collector*, January 2013.

[10]Sue White to Hu C. and Virginia Anderson, December 31, 1928, Sue Shelton White Papers, Schlesinger Library.

[11]Hu C. Anderson to Sue White, January 2, 1929, Sue Shelton White Papers, Schlesinger Library.

[12]Sue White to Virginia Anderson, undated, Sue Shelton White Papers, Schlesinger Library.

[13]Virginia Anderson to Sue White, March 2, 1929, Sue Shelton White Papers, Schlesinger Library.

[14]W.B. Hays affidavit draft, undated, Sue Shelton White Papers, Schlesinger Library.

[15]William A. White to Hu C. Anderson, December 21, 1931, Sue Shelton White Papers, Schlesinger Library.

[16]Hu C. Anderson to Sue White, December 26, 1931, Sue Shelton White Papers, Schlesinger Library.

[17]Sue White to Hu C. Anderson, December 11, 1931, Sue Shelton White Papers, Schlesinger Library.

[18]"Body of Mrs. Anderson to be Sent to Columbia," *Nashville Tennessean*, July 29, 1933.

[19]"Miss Etta L. Taggart Admitted to Bar," *Star-Gazette*, Elmira, New York, May 10, 1927.

[20]Etta L. Taggart to Sue White, May 1935, Sue Shelton White Papers, Schlesinger Library.

[21]Description of package delivered to Mrs. W.B. Hays, October 8, 1936, Sue Shelton White Papers, Schlesinger Library.

[22]"Judge Hu C. Anderson to Sit at Trials of Nazis in Germany," *The Jackson Sun*, October 17, 1947.

[23]"Judge Anderson Hurt in Fall Down Shaft," *The Jackson Sun*, May 5, 1953.

[24]"Judge Anderson Dies as Result of Fall; Rites to be Saturday," *The Jackson Sun*, May 8, 1953.

Chapter 6: Two Mules

[1]Lovene Harrington Miller v George Miller, *Minutes of Chancery Court of Madison County*, December 5, 1929, p. 471.

[2]Mrs. Annie Mathis v T.E. Mathis, *Minutes of Circuit Court of Madison County*, June 22, 1929, p. 340.

[3]Joe H. Alexander v J.C. Gately et al, *Minutes of Chancery Court of Madison County*, February 24, 1930, p. 548.

[4]W.H. Tarwater et al v W.F. Darby et al, *Minutes of Chancery Court of Madison County*, December 4, 1929, p 458.

[5]J.T. Gooch v J.F. Witherspoon et al, *Minutes of Chancery Court of Madison County*, October 9, 1931, p. 346.

Chapter 7: Determined to Foment a Rebellion

[1]"Neither Man Nor Woman Can be Rated as Superior," Sue White review of *Man and Woman: A Study of Secondary and Tertiary Sexual Characteristics* by Havelock Ellis, *Nashville Tennessean*, unknown date.

[2]"A Paragon of Virtues, One of the Chief Feminists of Her Time," Sue White review of *Abigail Adams* by Dorothie Bobbe, *Nashville Tennessean*, April 25, 1929.

[3]"A Woman Who Lived Loudly with Few of Her Acts Minor," Sue White review of *The Terrible Siren: Victoria Woodhull* by Emanie Sachs, *Nashville Tennessean,* January 13, 1929.

[4]"Cheerful Feminism," Sue White review of *The Family in the Making* by Mary Burt Messer, *Nashville Tennessean*, May 20, 1928.

Chapter 8: Lady Warrior

[1]Sue White to Mary Dewson, November 23, 1928, Sue Shelton White Papers, Schlesinger Library.

[2]Ross, "Comments on Sue White," Sue Shelton White Papers, Schlesinger Library.

[3]*United States Census* for Washington, D.C., 1930.

[4]"Sue White Quits Democratic National Committee Job," *Nashville Tennessean*, December 24, 1933.

[5]Nellie Tayloe Ross to Mary Dewson, April 1, 1933, Sue Shelton White Papers, Schlesinger Library.

[6]Ware, *Beyond Suffrage: Women in the New Deal*, p. 95-96.

[7]Armstrong, "Sue Shelton White (1887-1943)," Sue Shelton White Papers, Schlesinger Library.

[8]Ware, *Beyond Suffrage: Women in the New Deal*, p. 95-96.

[9]Jack B. Tate, "Sue White: An Appreciation," October 5, 1958, Sue Shelton White Papers, Schlesinger Library.

[10]Rosalie Moynahan, "Sue White – Practical Idealist," May 10, 1958, Sue Shelton White Papers, Schlesinger Library.

[11]*Practical Platform Speaking* Certificate, April 1941, Sue Shelton White Papers, Schlesinger Library.

Chapter 9: World at War

[1]"Miss Lucy Goode White, a San Francisco newspaper woman," *The Fourth Estate*, January 15, 1916.

[2]"Move to Prevent Registration Shown: Miss Sue White, State Chairman, Tells of Harm Done in State," *Nashville Tennessean*, October 19, 1917.

[3]Marshall White to Sue White, July 28, 1918, Sue Shelton White Papers, Schlesinger Library.

[4]Marshall White to Sue White, October 13, 1918, Sue Shelton White Papers, Schlesinger Library.

[5]"Japanese American Internment," *Encyclopedia Britannica*, January 22, 2020.

[6]Lucy White Schiller to Sue White, April 11, 1942, Sue Shelton White Papers, Schlesinger Library.

[7]Mary Butler to Sue White, January 10, 1943, Sue Shelton White Papers, Schlesinger Library.

Chapter 10: Finding Home

[1]Lucy Somerville Howorth, "Sue Shelton White, Recollections of Lucy Somerville Howorth," undated, Sue Shelton White Papers, Schlesinger Library.

[2]Elizabeth Spence, "Sue White," undated, Sue Shelton White Papers, Schlesinger Library.

[3]Armstrong, "Sue Shelton White (1887-1943)," Sue Shelton White Papers, Schlesinger Library.

Chapter 11: The Final Battle

[1]Medical notes, 1937-1938, Sue Shelton White Papers, Schlesinger Library.

[2]Armstrong, "Sue Shelton White (1887-1943)," Sue Shelton White Papers, Schlesinger Library.

[3]Edness Kimball Wilkins to Sue White, June 15, 1942, Sue Shelton White Papers, Schlesinger Library.

[4]Mary Butler to Sue White, August 2, 1942, Sue Shelton White Papers, Schlesinger Library.

[5]Eleanor Roosevelt to Sue White, August 25, 1942, Sue Shelton White Papers, Schlesinger Library.

[6]Mabel Vernon to Sue White, 1942 or 1943, Sue Shelton White Papers, Schlesinger Library.

[7]Lucy White Schiller to Florence Armstrong, May 14, 1942, Sue Shelton White Papers, Schlesinger Library.

[8]Marshall White to Sue White and Florence Armstrong, September 8, 1942, Sue Shelton White Papers, Schlesinger Library.

[9]Betty Gram Swing, "A Brief Accolade to Sue S. White, the Intrepid Feminist," 1959, Sue Shelton White Papers, Schlesinger Library.

[10]Armstrong, "Sue Shelton White (1887-1943)," Sue Shelton White Papers, Schlesinger Library.

Chapter 12: Whatever the Cost

[1]"Miss Sue White Chosen to Study Laws on Women, Former Tennessee Girl Codifying for National Woman's Party Inequalities and Discrimination Against Women in State Laws," *Nashville Tennessean*, December 26, 1920.

[2]Armstrong, "Sue Shelton White (1887-1943)," Sue Shelton White Papers, Schlesinger Library.

[3]"Legal Profession Calls Women, Says Ohio Judge at State Meet," *The Nashville Tennessean*, June 12, 1927.

[4]"An Approach to Solution of the Marriage Problem," Sue White review of *Marriage in the Modern Manner* by Ira S. Wile and Mary Day Winn, *Nashville Tennessean*, unknown date.

[5]"Tactics and Techniques of the National Woman's Party Suffrage Campaign," *American Memories*, Library of Congress.

[6]"Women Owe Debt to Pioneers of 1848, Says Sue White," newspaper unknown, 1923, Sue Shelton White Papers, Schlesinger Library.

Epilogue: Gaiety and Grief

[1]Moynahan, "Sue White – Practical Idealist," Sue Shelton White Papers, Schlesinger Library.

[2]"A Queen Not Quite Great Enough," Sue White review of *Queen Louise of Prussia* by Gertrude Aretez, *Nashville Tennessean*, September 1, 1929.

CPSIA information can be obtained
at www.ICGtesting.com
Printed in the USA
LVHW080521250220
648039LV00003BA/27